A Heart for Imbabura

Book 6 of the Junior Jaffray Collection of Missionary Stories

Written by Barbara Hibschman

Illustrated by Elynne Chudnovsky
Cover Design by Step One Design
Portrait by Karl Foster
Based on *A Heart for Imbabura* by Charles Shepson

CHRISTIAN PUBLICATIONS/Camp Hill, Pennsylvania

 The mark of vibrant faith

Christian Publications
Publishing House of The Christian
and Missionary Alliance
3825 Hartzdale Drive, Camp Hill, PA 17011

© 1992 by Christian Publications
All rights reserved
ISBN: 0-87509-487-2
Printed in the United States of America

92 93 94 95 96   5 4 3 2 1

Unless otherwise indicated, Scripture taken from the HOLY BIBLE: NEW INTERNATIONAL VERSION. Copyright © 1973, 1978, 1984 by the International Bible Society. Used by permission of Zondervan Bible Publishers.

Chapter 1

Evelyn Chooses to Serve God

"Beep! Beep!" honked the horn of the car in the driveway.

"They're here!" shouted Evelyn.

"I'm coming, but I can't find my Bible," answered Edwin.

"Oh, Edwin, you are always losing your things," scolded Evelyn. It was true—her brother could never find his things when he wanted them.

"Here it is! Oh, no. I forgot to memorize my Bible verse. Will you help me learn it?" asked Edwin.

"Sure. We can practice it on the way, but please hurry up," said Evelyn.

Evelyn and Edwin Rychner (pronounced Richner) lived on a farm in Minnesota. A church in a nearby town was having Vacation Bible School. Every day someone from that church drove out to take the Rychner children to Vacation Bible School.

Evelyn could hardly wait to get there. She loved going to Vacation

Bible School. There were happy songs, stories, memory verse time, things to make, games to play and lots of cookies.

One day at Vacation Bible School turned out to be the most important day in Evelyn's life. The teacher told the story of how Jesus died for the sins of the whole world. She asked the children if they wanted to receive Jesus into their hearts.

Evelyn raised her hand. Yes, she wanted to become God's child. She prayed and asked Jesus to forgive her of all the wrong things that she had ever done. Then she asked Jesus to come into her heart.

Evelyn was so happy. She knew Jesus was her Savior. She knew she was God's child because the Bible said so. She remembered one of her memory verses: ". . . to all who received him, to those who believed in his name, he gave the right to become children of God" (John 1:12).

That decision to ask Jesus into her heart would change Evelyn's life forever.

A few years later, Evelyn made another important decision. She went to some meetings where the speakers were missionaries who had gone all over the world to tell people about Jesus. The church was decorated with banners and flags. The missionaries were all dressed up in special costumes. Sometimes they talked in funny languages.

This was really a special night for Evelyn. She heard that God needed people to serve Him, people who would go and tell others about Him. She heard God saying to her, "Evelyn, I want you to be a missionary for me."

Evelyn knew this was the best thing she could do with her life. Yes, she wanted to tell everyone about Jesus. She wanted everyone to know how to become God's child. She wanted to obey God.

That night, Evelyn gave her life to God. She told Him she would go wherever He wanted her to go and tell people about Jesus.

Evelyn did become a missionary. She went to Ecuador, South America.

Evelyn chose to serve God, but God had chosen her first. Even before she was born, God had a plan for Evelyn's life. She would be His special messenger to the Indians in Ecuador, South America.

Chapter 2

Ecuador at Last

The first thing Evelyn noticed whe she arrived in Ecuador was that the people spoke Spanish. Evelyn had learned Spanish while she was still in the United States, so she could talk with them right away.

Even though Evelyn could understand and speak Spanish, she did not always think like an Ecuadorian. She had to learn the customs of the people in Ecuador. She had to learn that people in South America do not always do things like Americans or Canadians do them.

One day, Evelyn decided to have Vacation Bible School for the Spanish-speaking children. She remembered the day when she had given her heart to Christ at Vacation Bible School in Minnesota. She wanted other children to be able to do that, too.

Evelyn chose to have the meetings in a beautiful yard, under a big, shady tree.

Two Ecuadorian girls from the

church helped her set up the benches for the children to sit on. They put up the flannelgraph board and tuned the guitar. Soon, they were ready to start the meeting.

How will we get the children in the neighborhood to come? wondered Evelyn. Then she had an idea.

"Azucena, would you and your friend walk up and down the streets and ring the cowbell? Then the children will know that we are having Vacation Bible School and will come with you."

"Oh, no, Señorita. We can't do that," answered Azucena.

"Why not?" asked Evelyn. "There's nothing to it."

Both girls giggled and shook their heads back and forth as if to say no.

Evelyn didn't understand why they wouldn't do it. So she said, "All right, you stay here and I'll go ring the cowbell."

And that's what Evelyn did. She walked up and down the streets of the neighborhood ringing the cowbell. She called to the children, "Come, follow me to Vacation Bible School."

Soon there were lots of excited children under the big, shady tree in the beautiful backyard. Evelyn's two helpers were waiting for her when she got back. They were still giggling.

"How many people came running out with their garbage?" asked Azucena. "Do you know why we didn't want to ring the cowbell?"

The girls explained that it was their custom in Ecuador that only the garbage man rang a cowbell in the streets. It was his way of telling the people that he was there to take their trash away.

The children knew Evelyn didn't always understand how things were done in Ecuador, but they did know that Evelyn loved God and she loved them, too.

Later, when the children heard the Bible stories, they also knew God loved them.

CHAPTER 3

The Mountain with a Heart

Eem-bah-boo-rah. Can you say Eem-bah-boo-rah? That's right—Eem-bah-boo-rah.

Imbabura is the name of a big, high mountain in Ecuador. Usually clouds hide the beautiful snowy peak of the mountain, but sometimes you can see the top of it.

Mount Imbabura is a special mountain, because on one of its slopes you can see a valentine. Oh, it's not a big, red, paper valentine, but it's a place where there was a landslide that left a clearing the shape of a valentine. Can you see the valentine on the side of the mountain in the picture on the cover of the book?

What do you think of when you see a valentine or a heart? Most of us think of love. We may think of our mommies and daddies and how they love us. That's why God gave us families—to love and take care of us.

Or, we may remember God's

love for us and how He sent Jesus to be our Savior and Friend.

The Indians who lived around Mount Imbabura did not think of love when they saw the heart. Instead, they were afraid. They thought that bad spirits lived on the mountain.

The Indians were afraid of a lot of things.

They were afraid of thieves who might come into their houses and steal their things. There were lots of thieves in Ecuador. Sometimes, the people even slept outside so they would hear if someone was trying to steal their crops or their animals.

The Indians were also afraid of getting sick. If they got sick there was no place for them to go to get medicine. Oh yes, there was a hospital, but Indians were a different color than the rest of the people. They smelled different. They ate different foods. They spoke a different language. So they were not welcome at the hospital.

The biggest fear of all was when the Indians saw a rainbow. We think rainbows are beautiful, but the Indians were afraid of rainbows. They would beat on their pots and pans, hoping the loud noises would chase the rainbow away. They even pinched the ears of their dogs, hoping that the dogs' howling would make the rainbow go away.

Why were they so afraid of the rainbow?

They were afraid because they thought Satan had put it there. They did not know that the Bible says God put the rainbow in the sky as a sign of His love.

The Indians carry big loads on their backs when they go to market—loads of fruit, vegetables, clothing or other things they will sell at the market.

When Evelyn saw those awful, heavy loads on their backs she thought, *Those loads are very big and heavy but the Indians can put them down when they get to the market. I want to talk to them about another big load they carry. I want to tell them that the big load of fear they carry in their hearts can be put down, too. It can be given to the Lord Jesus Christ.*

Jesus came to take away everybody's fear, even the big load of fear in the hearts of the Indians of Imbabura.

Chapter 4

Evelyn Is in Trouble

"Tap, tap, tap," went the strange noise.

It was midnight and it was very, very dark outside. There it was again—that noise. Someone was tapping. It seemed like Evelyn could hear dirt falling, too. Were the noises coming from the garage?

Evelyn got out of bed and woke up her missionary friend, Marge. Evelyn and Marge lived together in the big Mission house in Imbabura. They listened, but they could not hear any strange noises. They couldn't see anything out the windows either. There were no lights anywhere.

Evelyn and Marge went back to bed, but Evelyn couldn't sleep. She knew the noises were not a dream or her imagination. She kept thinking, *Someone must be out in the garage.*

"Tap, tap, tap," went the strange noise again. This time Evelyn was sure the noises were coming from the garage.

"Marge, wake up! There are thieves in the garage," whispered Evelyn.

"Where's the key?" asked Marge.

"I've got it," Evelyn answered. "Let's sneak out the front door and see if we can surprise the thieves."

The women tiptoed to the front door. They unlocked it. But when they opened the door, the hinges squeaked. The thieves must have heard the noise, for by the time the women got to the garage, no one was there.

But what a surprise they found! There, in the wall, was a big hole where the thieves had taken away the mud bricks. Evidently, they thought they could steal some of the missionaries' things from the garage. The hole was just about big enough to get the big suitcases out.

Evelyn and Marge put the bricks in place and went back to bed. But Evelyn lay awake again. She was thinking. *This is my first night in Imbabura. This could be a very dangerous place for me to live. I hope the people back home are remembering to pray for me.*

Evelyn thought of something she had read in the Bible that very morning: "Do not fear, for I am with you." That verse helped Evelyn to remember that God was with her. She didn't need to be afraid. She went to sleep.

Yes, Imbabura was a dangerous place to live. Some of the Indians did not want the missionaries there. They did not want to hear the story of Jesus that Evelyn had come to tell them.

Another day, Evelyn was driving through a small town. The streets were very narrow and the houses were right on the edge of the streets.

Evelyn always took lots of little booklets along with her when she went on these trips. She would throw them out of the window as she drove by. The Indians were happy to have something to read. They would come running to pick up the little books. Sometimes, they would even sit down on the edge of the road and begin to read their copy right there.

On this day the people were not happy that Evelyn was passing through their village. They started throwing rocks and pieces of mud at Evelyn's jeep. Evelyn began to be afraid. Then she remembered the verse again: "Do not fear, for I am with you."

The next time she came through that town, she had a government official with her. He asked her to stop the jeep.

The man got out and told the villagers that they were not to throw things at Evelyn or her jeep anymore. He would personally see that they were punished if they did.

The next time Evelyn drove through that town, the people just glared at her. They still were not happy that she was there. They still did not want to hear her message about the Lord Jesus Christ.

But Evelyn was not afraid. God had told her not to be afraid. He was with her.

Chapter 5

The Box That Talked

One of the first people Evelyn met in Imbabura was Mama Manuela. Can you say her name? Mahn-way-lah.

As Evelyn walked up to the Mission house for the first time, Mama Manuela greeted her with a smile. Then she began to pray, "Dear Lord, bless this new missionary who has come to tell the Indians about Jesus."

Evelyn soon found out that Mama Manuela had not always known about Jesus or how to pray.

In fact, when Mama Manuela first came to the Mission house she was very sad. Her daughter, Josefa, had been sick. Daniel, Mama Manuela's son, begged his mother to take Josefa to the Mission clinic to get some medicine. But Mama Manuela was afraid to go to the Mission.

Instead, she went to visit the witchdoctors. They promised Mama Manuela that if she did

what they told her Josefa would get better.

But nothing helped Josefa. She became so weak, she died.

Mama Manuela became very sad. She was so sad that she decided to go to the clinic to see if the missionaries had some kind of medicine to take away her bad thoughts.

When Mama Manuela arrived at the clinic the missionaries told her that they did not have medicine to take away bad thoughts. But they knew a Person who could take away bad thoughts. God loved her so much, the missionaries said, that He sent Jesus to be her Savior and Friend. They explained that Jesus could take her sins away and give her a new life with happy thoughts.

That day, Mama Manuela asked the Lord Jesus to forgive all her sins. She asked Him to come into her heart to be her Savior. And from that day on, Mama Manuela was a different person. She became a happy person and wanted to tell everyone she met about her new life.

Mama Manuela began to come to the Mission house every day to help the missionaries. She ground coffee, husked corn and pulled weeds from the garden. And she also prayed—in the bedroom, with the door closed. She prayed for her Indian people that they would come to know Jesus.

Mama Manuela helped on clinic days, too. While the Indians waited to see the nurse, she told them Bible stories. And, if she knew sick people who couldn't come to the clinic, she took Evelyn to their homes to pray for them and give them medicine.

Sometimes Mama Manuela carried a record player on her back as they walked from house to house.

One day, as the women walked up to a house, Evelyn called out, "Lend me your path." That meant, "May I come in?"

A lady answered, "I lend you my path." That meant, "You're welcome to come and visit me."

Mama Manuela and Evelyn found an Indian woman squatting in her yard shelling corn. They squatted down, too, and shelled corn while they talked.

"Would you like to see what this box can do?" asked Mama Manuela.

The Indian woman answered, "Oh, yes, but what can a box do?"

The woman never dreamed that the box could talk! In fact, this box could even sing!

Evelyn put a record on the record player. Now, you know that music began to come out of the box. But the Indian woman was surprised to hear Indian songs being sung in her own language. They were happy songs that told of God's love for the Indians of Imbabura. She asked Evelyn to play the records over and over.

Mama Manuela and Evelyn became best friends. They loved to work together. They walked hundreds of miles all over Imbabura sharing God's love with the Indians through the box that talked.

Chapter 6

The Big Party

Have you ever gone shopping to buy a gift for someone special? Isn't it fun to pick something your friend will like? Something they will remember for a long time? We choose the best gifts for the people we love the most.

Evelyn liked to do that, too. She knew that someday she would have to leave Imbabura and go back to the United States. She wanted to give the Indians gifts that would not get old or wear out. She wanted to leave something that would last forever. Do you have an idea what kinds of gifts she gave them? You will be surprised at the gifts Evelyn chose.

The first gift was a songbook. The Indians spoke a different language from the other people in Ecuador, so Evelyn helped to write some songs for them to sing in their own language. She wanted them to be able to praise the Lord with words they could understand.

The more they sang the songs in the new book, the more they understood God's love for them. Evelyn knew that the gift of a songbook would last a long time because even if the songbooks wore out, the words of the songs would be in the hearts of the Indians. They could sing them over and over.

The second gift Evelyn gave the Indians was a message, a very special message that she wanted them to hear. The message said, "Jesus died for your sins, for all the wrong things you have done. If you will ask Him to forgive you, He will take your sins away and come into your heart."

Many Indians believed Evelyn's message and became Christians. Evelyn also told them that being baptized is a way to show others that you have asked Jesus into your heart. Have you ever seen someone baptized? Just like Jesus was baptized in a river, hundreds of Indians were baptized in the beautiful blue water of Lake San Pablo at the base of Mount Imbabura.

Pastors and elders helped the people walk into the lake, while friends and family stayed on the shore to watch. One by one the Indians told how they had asked Jesus into their hearts. Then the pastor baptized them by dipping each one under the water and raising them up again.

Going under the water reminded the Indians that their sins were washed away. Coming out of the water reminded them of the new life they were beginning because the Lord Jesus was their Savior.

The third gift Evelyn gave the Indians of Imbabura was the New Testament in their own language. It took a lot of work to make sure that the Indian Bible said the same things that the English Bible said. Every word had to be checked to make sure it was just right. Do you want to see what some of the Indians' words looked like? *Tigrachishpa, yacunaiyan, shuj shuhua.* They sure look a lot different than our words, don't they? When all the words were right, the pages were sent to a printer and made into books.

This gift was so special that Evelyn and the Indians decided to have a big celebration to let everyone know that the New Testament had finally arrived.

It was such an exciting day. The Indians got all dressed up in their colorful clothes. Large groups of them came singing and carrying banners covered with flowers. Church choirs sang and a band played. Speeches were made, and of course, there was lots of food.

What a big party it was! There were over 1,000 people at the party!

Giving the Indians the New Testament in their own language was a gift that would last forever. They would have the story of God's love as long as they read and obeyed His Word.

When Evelyn went back home to the United States the Indians all thanked her for the wonderful gifts she had given them. They knew that she loved them very much.

And, they had heard and believed her special message—that God loved them, too.

THE JUNIOR JAFFRAY
COLLECTION OF MISSIONARY STORIES
For additional copies of *A Heart for Imbabura* or information about other titles in the **Junior Jaffray Collection of Missionary Stories**, contact your local Christian bookstore or call Christian Publications toll-free at 1-800-233-4443

*Titles coincide with the adult biography series, **The Jaffray Collection of Missionary Portraits.**